Building a Tree Fort

Measure Lengths in Standard Units

Will Nelson

INFOMAX MATH READERS

Rosen Classroom™

New York

Published in 2015 by The Rosen Publishing Group, Inc.
29 East 21st Street, New York, NY 10010

Book Design: Jonathan J. D'Rozario

Photo Credits: Cover, p. 22 Ron Zmiri/Shutterstock.com; p. 5 Johner/Johner Images/Getty Images; pp. 7, 9 (wood background) Pavel L Photo and Video/Shutterstock.com; p. 7 (ruler) Vidux/Shutterstock.com; pp. 7, 11, 15, 21 (measuring tape) romvo/Shutterstock.com; p. 9 (hammer) Ruslan Semichev/Shutterstock.com; p. 9 (level) Ieva Geneviciene/Shutterstock.com; p. 9 (ruler) SmileStudio/Shutterstock.com; pp. 11, 15, 17, 19, 21 (grass) Tungphoto/Shutterstock.com; pp. 11, 15, 21 (yellow tape) phoelix/Shutterstock.com; pp. 11 (truck) tele52/Shutterstock.com; pp. 11, 15, 17, 19 (wood) Luca_Luppi/Shutterstock.com; p. 13 (background) Andrey Ezhov/Shutterstock.com; pp. 13, 19 (yard stick) Zedcor Wholly Owned/Thinkstock.com; p. 17 (background) PremiumVector/Shutterstock.com; p. 21(background) PILart/Shutterstock.com.

ISBN: 978-1-4777-4782-7
6-pack ISBN: 978-1-4777-4780-3

Manufactured in the United States of America

CPSIA Compliance Information: Batch #WS15RC: For further information contact Rosen Publishing, New York, New York at 1-800-237-9932.

Contents

Tree Fort Fun

Have you ever played in a tree fort? Tree forts are built between the trunk and branches of a tree. They can be great hideouts!

Some tree forts are simple and have only a **platform** and deck to sit on. Others are like small houses, and they can have a room, roof, and even windows. Some tree forts are only a few feet off the ground, while others are way up in a tree.

With the help of an adult, you can build your own tree fort! Building is good practice for measuring length.

Tools

You'll need tools for measuring and tools for building. To measure an object that's 1 foot or less, you can use a ruler. Rulers are 1 foot long. If an object is 3 feet (91.4 centimeters) or less, you can use a yardstick or meter stick. They're both around the same length. For objects longer than 3 feet, use a measuring tape.

Yardsticks use **U.S. standard** units, such as inches, feet, and yards. A yardstick is 3 feet, or 1 yard, long. Meter sticks use **metric** units, such as centimeters and meters. Rulers often have U.S. standard units on one side and metric units on the other.

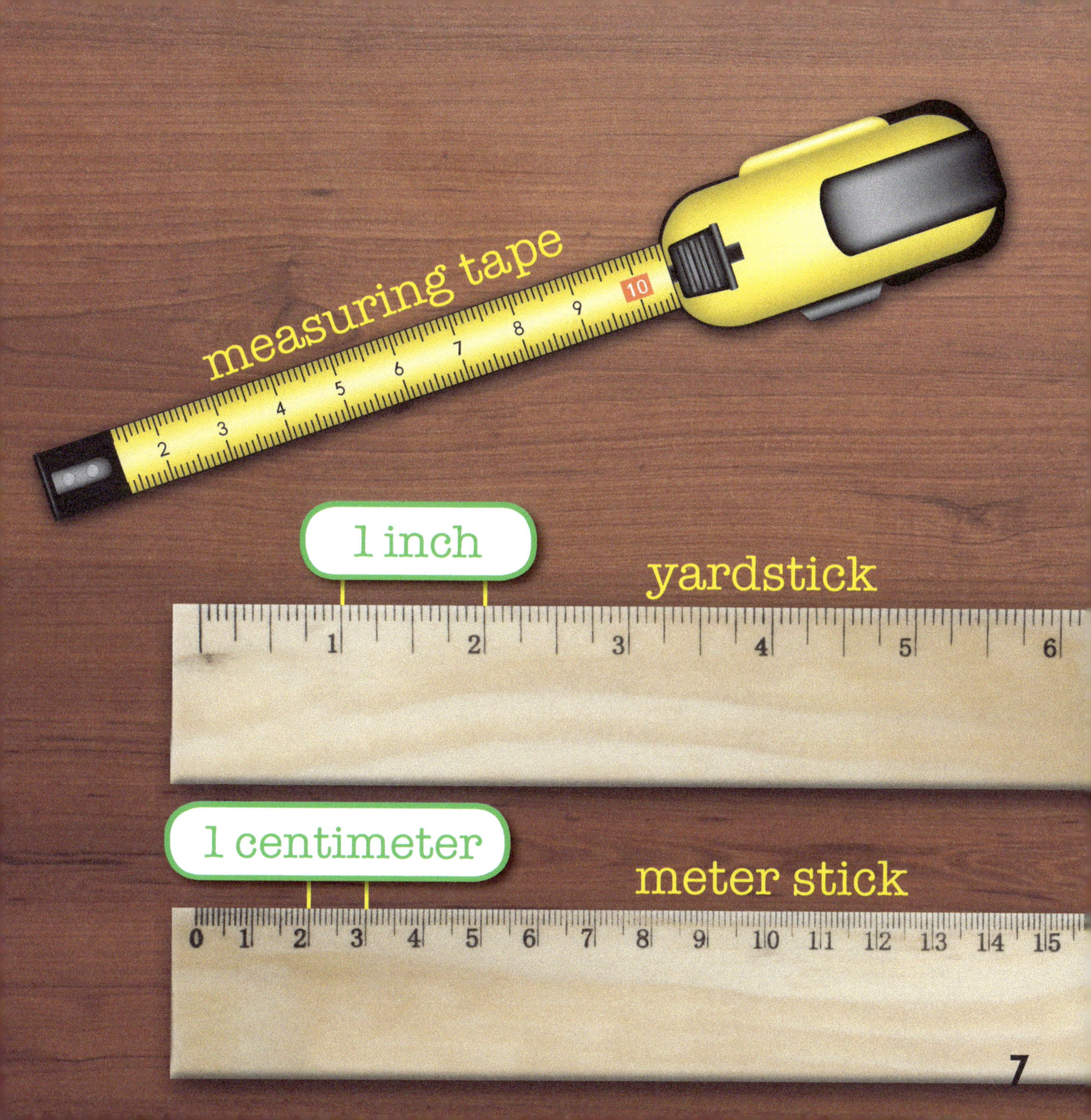
measuring tape
1 inch
yardstick
1 centimeter
meter stick

Important tools for building are hammers, saws, drills, and levels. Hammers and drills punch nails or screws into wood. Saws cut wood to the length that's needed.

Levels are tools that have a glass **tube** with a bubble. When the level is held straight, the bubble rests in the middle of the tube. This tells builders if objects are perfectly level.

You can measure the lengths of your building tools. This hammer looks like it's about 1 foot long, so you can use a ruler to measure it. It's 11 inches long.

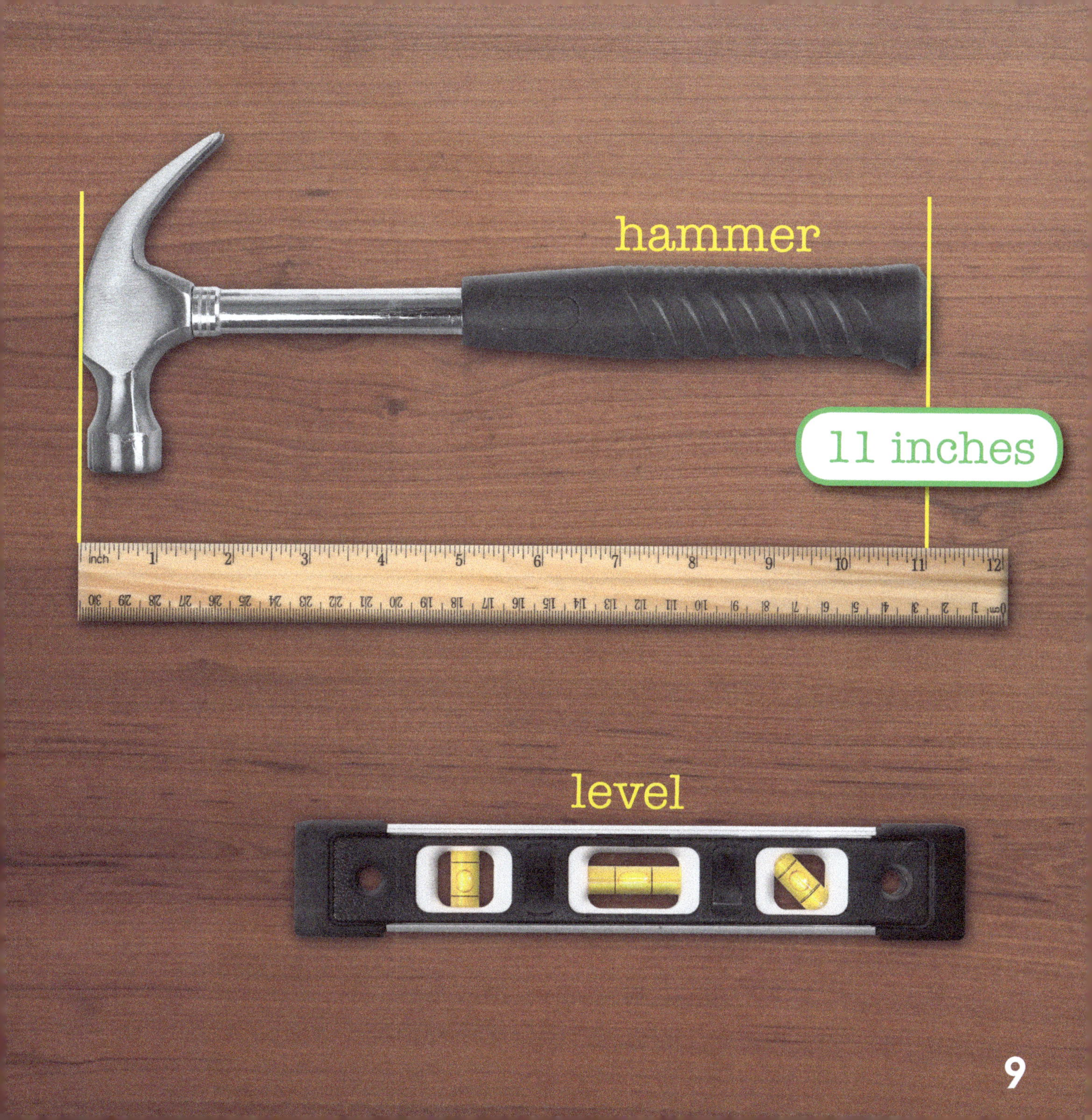
hammer
11 inches
level

Building Supplies

Your building supplies for a tree fort should include wooden boards. The boards must be different lengths because each board is used for a certain part of the fort.

If you want your platform to be 9 feet long, you'll need boards that are 9 feet long. Which tool should you use to measure a 9-foot board? Use a measuring tape!

It's important to measure an object using a tool that's longer than the object. That way, you won't have to move the tool while measuring, which can make the measurement incorrect.

9 feet

The Perfect Tree

You can't make a tree fort without the perfect tree. You need to find a tree that has a trunk and branches that are strong and solid. The tree should be healthy and alive.

You can build a tree fort on just 1 tree if it has strong branches and you want a smaller tree fort. Or you can use more than 1 tree to make a bigger tree fort.

If you're using more than one tree, the trees must be close enough. If you want trees that are 3 feet (91.4 cm) apart or less, which tools could you use to measure? Yardsticks and meter sticks!

3 feet

Getting Started

Each tree fort is built differently, but each should have a written set of plans before it's built. For many tree forts, the first step in building is to **secure** the supports to the tree.

Support boards are nailed into the tree and help to hold the weight of the fort. Suppose you are using 6-foot support boards. What should you use to measure them?

If you guessed a measuring tape, you're right! Measuring tapes can be 12 feet long or even longer. They're made out of cloth, metal, or plastic. The longest measuring tape in the world is 600 feet (183 m) long!

6 feet

The next step is usually building the platform. The platform supports the deck, or the floor of the tree fort. If you want 8-foot boards for this, use a measuring tape to get an **accurate** measurement.

After the platform is secured in the tree, you'll build the deck. The deck should be cut to fit around the tree trunks or limbs.

You should leave a few inches between the deck and the tree so the tree can grow. If you want to measure 3 inches, what tool would you use? Remember that it's important to start at 0!

3 inches

Safety First

Some tree forts have railings to make them safer. If you want your railing to be 34 inches from the deck, you could use a yardstick to measure.

After you cut the wood, measure it with a meter stick to find out the metric measurement. You'll find that 34 inches equals about 86 centimeters. Why is it useful to know both metric and U.S. standard units?

Metric units are used all over the world, but U.S. standard units are only used in a few countries, such as the United States.

34 inches

To make it easy to climb in and out of your tree fort, you can buy or build a ladder. The ladder has to be equal to or greater than the distance between the deck and the ground. If your tree fort is 5 feet off the ground, the ladder should be 5 feet long or longer. Which tool would you use to measure a ladder for this fort?

Some tree forts use wooden or metal ladders. Others have rope ladders or sometimes just a rope. No matter what kind you use, it's important to measure the length correctly.

5 feet

Plan Your Own!

The most important part about building a tree fort is to make it your own! You might only build a deck and a railing. However, if you want a room, you could build one on top of the deck. Some tree forts even have more than 1 room.

Tree forts, big or small, can be the best places to play when you're outside!

What kind of tree fort would you like to build? Draw a plan for one and think about the lengths of the supplies you'll use.

Glossary

accurate (AA-kyuh-ruht) Free of mistakes.

metric (MEH-trihk) Units of measurement used worldwide, which include centimeters, meters, and kilometers.

platform (PLAT-fohrm) A flat, raised surface used as a place to stand or put things.

secure (sih-KYUR) To attach firmly.

tube (TOOB) A long, hollow object that can carry a liquid or gas.

U.S. standard (YOO ESS STAN-duhrd) Units of measurement commonly used in the United States, which include feet, inches, and yards.

Index